Korean Pop Culture

THE NEW GLOBAL OBSESSION

John Allen

San Diego, CA

About the Author

John Allen is a writer who lives in Oklahoma City.

Printed in the United States

For more information, contact:
ReferencePoint Press, Inc.
PO Box 27779
San Diego, CA 92198
www.ReferencePointPress.com

LIBRARY OF CONGRESS CATALOGING-IN-PUBLICATION DATA

Author: John Allen -1957
Title: Korean Pop Culture: The New Global Obsession
Description: San Diego, CA : ReferencePoint Press, 2026.
Includes bibliographical references and index
Identifiers: LCCN 2025012803 (print) | ISBN 9781678210885 library binding | ISBN 9781678210892 ebook

For compete cataloging-in-publication data please go to www.loc.gov.

CONTENTS

A Newly Energized Pop Culture

Fans of so-called K-dramas, or South Korean–made television dramas, spend hours watching their favorite characters navigate the bizarre plot twists in each episode. They also tend to focus on what the characters are wearing. Oversized eyeglasses, scarves, bucket hats, and shirts and blouses in wild patterns—each detail says something about the characters and their unique personality. Inevitably, many fans decide to model their own style on their heroes' fashions. They seek out web retailers where these stylish items can be purchased. Using phone apps, fans can snap screenshots of fashion items on K-dramas and locate them online in seconds.

This kind of synergy—with the popularity of K-dramas boosting sales of clothes and accessories—is a major feature of Korean pop culture today. "One of the most notable aspects of dressing up after watching K-dramas is the attention to detail," says Karin, a follower of social media trends on the website Medium. "Viewers are inspired to pay more attention to accessories, layering, and color coordination. Whether it's a statement necklace, a stylish scarf, or a perfectly tailored blazer, K-drama fashion encourages viewers to experiment with their wardrobe and express their individuality through clothing."[1]

Popular Culture as a Major Export

Fans also love seeing their favorite pop singers turn up on K-dramas and hearing the latest K-pop hits on the soundtrack. Many of South Korea's pop music idols have launched successful acting careers, playing everything from romantic leads to supporting roles. News of a pop star's appearance—as when Jisoo of the group Blackpink starred in the romantic drama series *Snowdrop*—guarantees an avalanche of fan base reviews and social media posts.

All this excitement and activity has helped transform South Korea into a thriving center for pop culture worldwide. Its success as an exporter of pop culture is even more surprising in view of the obstacles it has had to overcome. Fifty years ago South Korea was one of the world's poorest nations. Many areas lacked reliable electric power and indoor plumbing. Its economy even lagged behind that of Communist North Korea, with whom it shared a tense border arrangement. Political freedom in South Korea took a back seat to questions of how to feed the population and create jobs.

In the 1980s and 1990s, Korean leaders began to seek new paths to prosperity. The government offered support to entertainment corporations, including money and resources. Korean movies,

Many of South Korea's pop music idols have launched successful acting careers. Among them are Blackpink's Jisoo, who appears here in a scene from the first season of the romantic drama series Snowdrop.

television dramas, and pop music attracted fans in Asia and eventually throughout the world. Leaders in government and business saw the promotion of South Korea's lively pop culture as a form of soft power—spreading influence without resorting to force. The effort became so successful that it was given a name: *Hallyu*, or the Korean Wave. As former president Moon Jae-in said in a 2019 speech, "When I meet with foreign nationals, I can sense their favorable impressions of Korea have grown."[2]

Irresistible Energy and Creativity

The Korean Wave of pop culture is marked by a creative exuberance that fans find hard to resist. K-pop groups produce catchy music in a variety of genres, from pop to rhythm and blues to electronic dance. Their music videos often feature elaborate visuals and choreography, with dance steps that fans are quick to imitate. K-dramas are known for their intricate storylines and shocking plot twists that keep the audience riveted. Furnishings and fashions are carefully chosen to suit the young characters' lifestyle. Most K-dramas focus on relatable themes such as friends and family relationships, love, and personal growth. Some productions explore fantasy and science-fiction territory, such as the wildly popular series *Squid Game*, about a deadly competition for a fabulous cash prize.

Korean pop music and dramas have managed to conquer the American market despite not being in English. The singing group BTS has produced several number one albums on the US *Billboard* 200 chart. The group's 2020 album *Map of the Soul: 7* sold more than 4 million copies in nine days. K-pop acts such as Stray Kids, Tomorrow X Together, and NewJeans have also had chart-topping hits around the world. Many K-dramas—including *Queen of Tears*, *True Beauty*, and *Doctor Slump*—were among the most-watched series on Netflix in 2024. *Parasite*, a feature film by the South Korean director Bong Joon-Ho, won the 2020 Academy Award for Best Picture. It became the first foreign-language film to win the award.

That cultural energy has moved beyond the entertainment industry. Korean fashion designers manage to fuse elegance with fanciful ideas. Cosmetics made in South Korea are considered among the world's finest. And Korean cuisine, with chefs combining traditional dishes with foods from other nations, has become a cutting edge favorite for adventurous diners worldwide.

"What began as the illustrious power of influence in Hallyu now leads the industrious might of South Korean innovation. All that's left is the question: what's next?"[3]

—Jack Neighbour, cultural writer for *National Geographic*

All this activity on the cultural front has enriched the Korean economy. South Korea's Ministry of Foreign Affairs estimates that in 2024, exports of Hallyu-related products and services brought in the equivalent of US$14.16 billion. The number of Hallyu fans around the world has surpassed 225 million and continues to grow. Today South Korea is widely seen as a futuristic haven for pop culture and exciting new ideas. "What began as the illustrious power of influence in Hallyu now leads the industrious might of South Korean innovation," says *National Geographic*'s Jack Neighbour. "All that's left is the question: what's next?"[3]

Riding the Korean Wave

Beginning in March 2024, visitors to the Museum of Fine Arts (MFA) in Boston, Massachusetts, were greeted by a pink tuxedo jacket at the entrance to a brand-new installation. For those in the know, the jacket brought back memories of a twelve-year-old music video that had taken the pop world by storm. For the video of his 2012 hit song "Gangnam Style," the rapper-dancer PSY had worn the jacket, among other outfits, while performing his whimsical side-to-side dance, which resembled riding an invisible horse. Young people all over the world had watched the video countless times and tried to copy its dance steps. "Gangnam Style," named for a glamorous, upscale district in Seoul, South Korea, brought a message of pure fun to popular culture of the early 2010s. Sung in a mixture of English and Korean, it also announced that Korean pop music, or K-pop, was poised to challenge the biggest acts of the music business.

The MFA installation, called *Hallyu! The Korean Wave*, served to spotlight South Korea's pop culture explosion and its rising influence in the world. The exhibit included more than two hundred costumes and artifacts from pop bands, music videos, television dramas, and feature films. One display re-created the bathroom set from the Oscar-winning Korean movie *Parasite*. Another featured the distinctive and ominous pink guard costumes and green tracksuits from the Netflix K-drama series *Squid Game*. The installation also presented examples of South Korean art, fashion, and beauty products. Before exiting the show, visitors could take part in an interactive dance challenge by trying the steps in an intricate K-pop dance video. "*Hallyu! The Korean Wave* is unlike any exhibition we've ever hosted at the MFA," said Matthew Teitelbaum, one of the museum's directors. "It brings a new energy and excitement to the Museum, while at the same time honoring our longstanding commitment to collecting and displaying Korean art."[4] Other major museums, such as the Art Institute of Chicago and the Victoria and Albert Museum in London, have also highlighted the Korean Wave with major exhibitions.

An Unlikely Path to Success

Just a few decades ago, such a cultural breakthrough on a global scale would have seemed highly unlikely for South Korea. In the 1950s and 1960s, the nation was struggling to recover from a

The South Korean rap-and-dance sensation, PSY, models his signature pink tuxedo in Paris in 2012. The tuxedo was part of a 2024 Boston museum exhibit highlighting South Korea's pop culture explosion and its rising influence in the world.

bloody war that left the Korean Peninsula divided between it and Communist North Korea. The South's economy faltered under an authoritarian government that blocked democratic reforms. The Hermit Kingdom, as South Korea was still called in those lean postwar years, was looked on as one of the world's poorest nations. But as conditions slowly improved, government leaders began to look for new ways to promote business activity across the nation. They backed the formation of huge chaebols, or conglomerates, each made up of several businesses owned by one individual or family. These powerhouse corporations included names such as Samsung, Hyundai, SK Group, and LG Electronics. Long overshadowed by China and Japan on the world stage, South Korea finally began to assert its own economic strength. Chaebols became the basis of the country's growth strategy. Even today they remain the backbone of South Korea's economy. In 2021

A Tense Relationship with North Korea

South Korea's Hallyu project to export its pop culture has had to negotiate serious conflict with its neighbor to the north, Communist North Korea. The 2.5-mile-wide (4 km) stretch of the demilitarized zone (DMZ) that separates the two nations is surrounded on both sides by some of the most heavily armed garrisons in the world. Kim Jong-un, the North's authoritarian ruler, has said he considers South Korea a foreign and hostile nation.

K-dramas have often featured plotlines about the relationship between the two countries. The romantic comedy series *Crash Landing on You* deals with a rich young female entrepreneur from the South who is blown across the DMZ in a paragliding accident. She ends up falling in love with a handsome North Korean border patrol officer who rescues her from a tree. In real life, South Korean activists have sent USB drives loaded with K-pop and K-dramas over the border via balloons to influence the North. However, North Koreans who are caught watching a K-drama can face imprisonment or death. According to Choi Kyong-hui, whose institute provides aid to defectors from the North, "You can see how wary the North Korean regime is about spreading and watching Korean dramas."

Quoted in Yoonjung Seo and Lucas Lilieholm, "Rare Footage Shows North Korean Teens Punished for Watching South Korean Dramas, Research Group Claims," CNN, January 24, 2024. www.cnn.com.

the top ten family-controlled chaebols produced 60 percent of the country's gross domestic product. And South Korea differs from many capitalist democracies in the level of cooperation between its large corporations and the government.

> **"[Former South Korean president Kim Dae-jung] marvelled [at] how much revenue the United States brought in from films and the UK from stage musicals. He decided to use those two countries as benchmarks for creating a pop culture industry in Korea."[5]**
>
> —Euny Hong, author of *The Birth of Korean Cool*

South Korean leaders looked to the future by aggressively pursuing technological advancement. The government created institutes for research and development. It helped finance industries that designed and manufactured computer chips. Due to years of investment in fiber-optic networks, South Korea boasted the world's fastest internet speeds, a distinction it maintains to this day. The government also eased travel restrictions for its citizens. This allowed Koreans to visit other countries, mainly the United States and European nations, and learn firsthand about other cultural traditions. Many young Koreans went to college in the West and got jobs there after graduation. When they returned home, they brought with them new perspectives on business and culture.

However, the government's most important—and perhaps most surprising—decision was to promote South Korea's popular culture, not only regionally but worldwide. Following a severe economic crash in 1997, Korean leaders were looking for ways to repair the country's reputation as a reliable place to do business. What was needed, according to then-president Kim Dae-jung, was a huge rebranding effort, a makeover for the nation. "Kim marvelled [at] how much revenue the United States brought in from films and the UK from stage musicals," writes Korean American journalist Euny Hong in her book *The Birth of Korean Cool*. "He decided to use those two countries as benchmarks for creating a pop culture industry in Korea."[5]

Kim reversed the way so-called soft power (or cultural power) is usually wielded by culturally dominant countries like the United

With South Korea's economy struggling in the late 1990s, then-president Kim Dae-jung (pictured in 2000) decided that his country needed a makeover. He embarked on a huge rebranding effort that led to the creation of Korea's pop culture industry.

States. He sought to place culture before economics, spreading the idea of "Korean cool" first and letting its benefits accrue to corporations like LG and Samsung later. And the positive economic impact of cultural products could be enormous. As pointed out in a 1994 report by the South Korean Presidential Advisory Council on Science & Technology, the American movie *Jurassic Park* made as much money in one year as Hyundai made from selling 1.5 million cars. Perhaps, thought South Korea's leaders, Korean filmmakers should be making blockbuster movies of their own.

Kim and his ministers plowed money and resources into a national office of cultural content. They also set up a public-private investment fund that poured billions into Korean creative businesses, including film studios, recording studios, and promotion agencies. They even boosted innovative businesses in food, fashion, and cosmetics. In a bid to locate musical talent, promoters launched singing competitions. In 2009 a new TV show called *Superstar K* (a version of *America's Got Talent*) received more than 700,000 applications to audition. Four years later the number had grown to 2 million. Some singers parlayed their success on *Superstar K* into recording contracts or roles in popular K-dramas.

Expanding the Audience

The best K-pop groups soon expanded their following beyond national borders. They began to attract fans in Japan, Indonesia, India, Pakistan, North Africa, and the Middle East. K-dramas managed to draw non-Korean audiences despite the language barrier. Korean cool soon proved to be more than just a marketing idea. As Hong notes, "[Government leaders] decided that Korea was going to be the coolest country in the world—the only non-English-speaking nation ever to successfully export its pop culture."[6]

To reach a wider audience, entertainment companies focused on work that was fresh, colorful, and fun. Often, they had to push back against South Korea's traditional culture to create more modern content. Whereas much of Korea's popular music used to be melancholy and unfit for dancing, producers of K-pop focused on Western musical styles that were upbeat and highly danceable. The government eased its formerly stiff standards of censorship, enabling K-dramas to explore more adult themes and appeal to a wider audience. The new approach even extended to products like cosmetics. Makeup, lip balms, and moisturizers that had been sold in bland tubs and bottles were repackaged in quirky containers shaped like cartoon cats, walruses, or octopi. Loyal customers overseas loved the whimsical approach to marketing as well as the excellent products.

Ultimately, a major goal for the Korean Wave was to make cultural inroads in the richest market of all: the United States. In 2012 the lovably eccentric hip hop song and video "Gangnam Style" became a global sensation, including in America. The song's tongue-in-cheek send-up of a trendy district in South Korea's capital city of Seoul portrayed Korean pop culture as hip and full of fun. It also showed that irony and irreverence were not exclusive to Western pop culture. The creator of "Gangnam Style," rapper and songwriter

PSY (real name: Park Jae-sang), was the son of a Korean business executive and recorded for YG Entertainment, one of the largest music companies in Korea. His video became the first in YouTube history to achieve 1 billion views. The music press in America hailed the emergence of a new Asian star, with *Rolling Stone* magazine dubbing PSY "Seoul Brother No. 1."[7]

> **"[PSY] proved to everybody that instead of a Korean version of a Western pop star or an international pop star, what the world wanted was something very authentic, original, unique."[8]**
>
> **—Bernie Cho, president of the Seoul-based DFSB Kollective agency**

PSY's breakthrough with "Gangnam Style" continues to resonate through the Korean entertainment business today. Bernie Cho, president of the Seoul-based DFSB Kollective agency and an expert on the South Korean music industry, says that PSY

> broke the rules of the game. The traditional marketing and promotional playbooks were essentially thrown out the window. . . . Industry executives, government officials, pundits, critics, fans . . . just assumed that the breakout star from Korea would likely be either a boy band or a girl band. [PSY] proved to everybody that instead of a Korean version of a Western pop star or an international pop star, what the world wanted was something very authentic, original, unique.[8]

PSY not only broke down language and cultural barriers with the song. He also demonstrated the financial possibilities for K-pop. With its current tally of more than 5.5 billion views on YouTube, the video for "Gangnam Style" continues to add to the rapper's bank account. PSY has an estimated net worth today of more than $60 million.

Embracing Technology and the Hurry-Hurry Culture

By the mid-2010s the arrival of new K-pop groups, K-dramas, and K-products of all descriptions had become a flood—or a tidal wave. Songs by K-pop bands such as BTS, EXO, Red Velvet, Blackpink, Seventeen, Stray Kids, GFriend, and Twice rocketed up the world music charts. Many of these groups sold out concert halls in Asia, Europe, and the United States. In 2021–2022, BTS's combined album sales, streams, and downloads made them the world's best-selling music act, outselling even Taylor Swift. Meanwhile, K-dramas became a staple on Netflix, Hulu, and other streaming services worldwide. Fashion, food, and beauty products from South Korea gained a reputation for innovation and quality. As a 2022 headline in the British newspaper the *Guardian* put it, the world has embraced "K-Everything: The Rise and Rise of Korean Culture."[9]

Entertainment companies in South Korea have become adept at using the latest technology to promote pop culture and keep fans engaged. As smartphone use grew to dominate teen culture in Korea, companies turned to social media as their most

Sparing No Expense to Promote the Korean Wave

It is no secret that South Korea's government spares no expense in exporting Korean pop culture around the world. One of its key tools for this project is the Korea Creative Content Agency (KOCCA), which is part of the Ministry of Culture. "There are various subunits that include internet comics, design, dramas, music, cuisine, graphics, and animations," says Mutlu Binark, a professor of pop culture studies at Hacettepe University in Turkey. With a staggering budget of more than $5.5 billion, KOCCA plays a crucial role in promoting and sustaining the Korean Wave. It conducts detailed studies of the target audience for various cultural industries, with an emphasis on Asian nations. Its various divisions work to decide which products of the Korean Wave would fit best in different markets. Analysts agree that no one understands foreign cultural markets like South Korea.

The government also stages cultural festivals in other countries to exhibit Korean Wave offerings. High-powered public relations campaigns try to convey Korea's unique qualities. The government also has built a theme park for K-culture in Goyang, South Korea. And there is more to come. In 2023 the Korean government announced massive funding for 5G augmented reality technologies. According to Binark, "They call it the 'Digital Renaissance.'"

Quoted in Sumeyye Dilara Dincer, "From Cultural Phenomenon to State Strategy: South Korea's 'Hallyu Policy,'" Anadolu Agency, August 22, 2023. www.aa.com.

powerful promotional tool. So-called teaser video clips or images appear on social media weeks or months ahead of a group's new album release. This serves to build anticipation among fans eager for new music. Contests and giveaways are announced on TikTok and Instagram, along with news about a band's latest tour. Some companies specialize in cryptic social media posts that leave fans guessing about their true meaning. News about collaborations among bands or artists or a band member's upcoming appearance in a K-drama can guarantee a large audience for a new album or TV series.

Companies also pursue a strategy of immersive technology, to make fans feel closer to their favorite bands. Mobile games linked to K-pop groups might include special content for fans, such as pop-up offers for concert tickets. Recently, the K-pop industry has introduced virtual reality (VR) options for concert viewing. Fans can don VR headsets and watch live concerts as

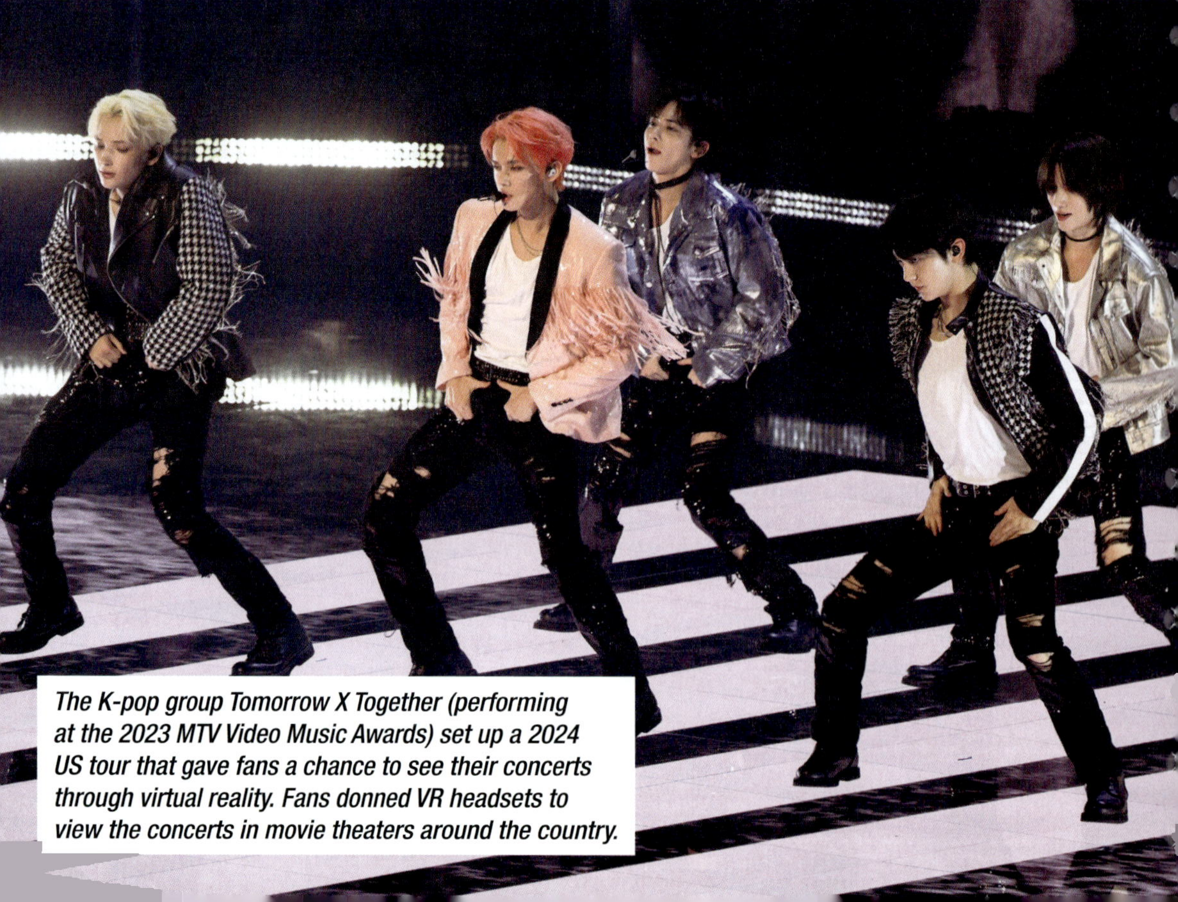

The K-pop group Tomorrow X Together (performing at the 2023 MTV Video Music Awards) set up a 2024 US tour that gave fans a chance to see their concerts through virtual reality. Fans donned VR headsets to view the concerts in movie theaters around the country.

if they were in the front row or even onstage with the band. In 2024 the K-pop group Tomorrow X Together set up an American tour in which fans in different cities watched a prerecorded concert on VR in movie theaters.

> "Palipali culture is an extremely powerful tool. It's a big part of what makes Korea do things that other countries can't—this characteristic of how we can all gang up together very quickly and get excited."[10]
>
> —Yoon Sooyeon, an orchestra musician in Seoul

Another aspect of the Korean Wave is its emphasis on speed, energy, and immediacy. Some pundits have noted how South Korea, once known as the Land of Morning Calm, has become a nation that hates to waste time. There is even a name for it in Korean: *palipali*, or hurry-hurry culture. It enables people to overcome obstacles and get things done. Street rallies in Seoul have even relied on it to defend South Korea's democracy. "Palipali culture is an extremely powerful tool," says Yoon Sooyeon, a forty-one-year-old orchestra musician in Seoul. "It's a big part of what makes Korea do things that other countries can't—this characteristic of how we can all gang up together very quickly and get excited."[10] With so much energy to spare, it seems likely that the pop culture Korean Wave is still on the rise.

The Explosion of K-Pop

In March 2024 several backstage photos posted on Instagram sent shock waves through two large fan bases. Following her Eras Tour concert on an outdoor stage in Kallang, Singapore, American singer-songwriter Taylor Swift was visited backstage by Lisa, a member of the K-pop group Blackpink. Swift had donned an old sweatshirt after her evening's work, while Lisa—whose real name is Lalisa Manobal—wore a punkish black bra and fishnet outfit. The two stars chatted and posed for snapshots that quickly went viral. Taylor's Swifties shared the excitement with Lisa's Blinks (the name for Blackpink fans). Lisa admitted on Instagram that she had had a blast at the concert and was thrilled to meet Swift after the show. She also displayed the friendship bracelets she had traded with Swift fans. Many of Lisa's 101 million Instagram followers could hardly contain their excitement about their idols' meeting and their pictures. "The power this picture [has] is crazy, biggest kpop artist and biggest artist in the world,"[11] wrote one of her fans. And another simply gushed, "It's real i'm crying."[12]

K-Pop's Appeal for Young People

K-pop groups like Blackpink have won over their fans with an irresistible mixture of catchy tunes, flashy choreography, cutting edge fashion, and colorful video productions. K-pop borrows from all sorts of musical styles, especially American genres like hip hop, rhythm and blues, rock, jazz, electronic dance, and synth-pop. It offers so many different varieties that there is a

K-pop group or performer for every musical taste. Groups often bounce between styles on their albums—and sometimes within individual songs. However, most K-pop is aimed at the dance floor, with a hypnotic beat, layered vocals, and glossy, high-sheen production values. Videos tend to feature an ever-changing montage of colorful backdrops, such as a royal palace in Thailand, a boulevard in Seoul, or a dance hall in a rustic village. And the focus on choreography can be mesmerizing, with group members performing dance moves in perfect synchronicity.

Although K-pop tunes are often upbeat and fun, many of them also deal with serious issues. Lyrics might explore personal struggles, loneliness, mental health, social injustice, the environment, and world peace. Fans identify with their K-pop idols, combing through their lyrics for hints about their private lives and personal beliefs. All these elements contribute to K-pop's strong appeal to young people. Fans love to spend hours discussing their favorite groups and videos on social media.

In the 1990s Korean entertainment companies launched the K-pop movement with a focus on what appealed to young listeners. Leading the first generation of K-pop idols was SM Entertainment's group H.O.T., made up of trained teenage pop performers

K-pop groups like Blackpink (pictured in 2022) have won over fans with an irresistible mix of catchy tunes, flashy choreography, cutting edge fashion, and colorful video productions.

with movie-star looks. The group's name was an acronym for High Five of Teenagers. Their 1997 hit "Candy" combined a catchy bubblegum tune with a bouncy dance beat. In the music video for "Candy," the five H.O.T. singers rocked colorful oversize sweats that became a fashion must-have for fans. For the next decade, other K-pop acts—including Bigbang, g.o.d (Groove Over Dose), and S.E.S.—used a similar formula for chart success. K-pop artists, commonly referred to as idols, began to gather a fan base that rivaled the audience for American boy bands such as the Backstreet Boys and NSYNC. Some critics complained that these groups lacked soul, having been manufactured by Korean producers and promoters strictly to compete with foreign music acts. Nonetheless, K-pop began its steady rise to musical prominence. As an analysis of K-pop on the Los Angeles Film School website explains, "The music industry loves a group of young people that can sing, dance, and appeal to consumers between the ages of 13–18. K-pop is the British Invasion for Gen Z but dialed up past 11. Not only are K-pop idols covering magazines and selling merch, but they are extraordinarily talented, perfectly styled, socially conscious, and capable of generating enormous engagement on social media."[13]

"The music industry loves a group of young people that can sing, dance, and appeal to consumers between the ages of 13–18. . . . Not only are K-pop idols . . . selling merch, but they are extraordinarily talented, perfectly styled, socially conscious, and capable of generating enormous engagement on social media."[13]

—Los Angeles Film School website

The BTS Hit-Making Phenomenon

In 2012, PSY's worldwide smash hit, "Gangnam Style," set the stage for many other K-pop acts to reach a global audience. By far the most successful of these was the boy group BTS, which debuted just one year after PSY's breakout. BTS was the brainchild of producer-songwriter Bang Si-Hyuk, head of the K-pop label Big Hit Entertainment. Bang recruited young performers who showed promise and then subjected them to months or sometimes years of grueling tutelage in singing and dancing. He also trained them in how to dress, be punctual, and comport themselves in public, much like Berry Gordy's Motown Records hit factory had done in 1960s Detroit, Michigan. The seven-member BTS, with three rappers and four vocalists, became Bang's prize achievement. They topped the music charts with a series of catchy dance tunes and edgy choreographed videos. Fans swooned over the group's smooth-cheeked good looks (aided by Korean skin care products), boyish enthusiasm, and impeccable dance moves.

The group also displayed a more thoughtful and introspective side that was characteristic of K-pop's next generation. Often called the Bangtan Boys, the group's name in Korean is *Bangtan Sonyeondan*, or Bulletproof Boy Scouts. Band member J-Hope explained that the name refers to how the group tries to block out stereotypes and criticisms that can target adolescents like bullets. BTS's debut single, "No More Dream," focused on young

A K-Pop Band with Hearing Problems Visits a School for the Deaf

A common theme of today's K-pop is reaching out to people and helping those who feel neglected or isolated. In this spirit, the group Big Ocean joined with the New York Police Department (NYPD) to visit kids at St. Joseph's School for the Deaf in the Bronx. All three members of Big Ocean—Lee Chan-yeon, Park Hyun-jin, and Kim Ji-seok—are themselves hearing impaired and can relate to the challenges deaf children face. When they learned of the NYPD's efforts to support the deaf and hard-of-hearing community, Big Ocean reached out to the department to deliver a message of hope to St. Joseph's.

Hyun-jin and Chan-yeon both lost their hearing in childhood but later had cochlear implant surgery. Ji-seok, Big Ocean's youngest member, was born with hearing problems. At St. Joseph's, the band's use of American Sign Language drew big smiles from the students. One girl pointed to Chan-yeon's hearing device, which was like hers. "We are so happy to see all of these kids who have the same type of disability we have," said Ji-seok, "and I wanted them to see our performance and learn how to grow and pursue their dream, whatever they are dreaming now."

Quoted in Amanda Moses, "NYPD Teams Up with Big Ocean, K-Pop First Hard-of-Hearing Act for Surprise Visit to Bronx School for Deaf Children," *AMNY*, November 13, 2024. www.amny.com.

people's anxiety in the face of high parental expectations. It was a meaningful theme for young listeners feeling classroom pressures every day. BTS became known not only for their old-school hip hop energy but also their realistic lyrics that deal with genuine teen frustrations. "Since their debut, BTS has always urged youths to think for themselves," says pop culture pundit Tiffany Yep. "Many young people can relate to the idea of lacking a dream that's truly their own."[14]

Soon BTS was racking up one K-pop success after another. In 2018 the group's album *Love Yourself: Tear* became their first to reach number one on the *Billboard* 200. Later that year, BTS gave a speech to the United Nations general assembly on the group's Generation Unlimited program to boost youth education and empowerment. In 2019 *Time* magazine listed the group among the one hundred most influential people of the year. That summer, they became the first K-pop group to perform on *Saturday Night Live*, as well as the first to perform at London's Wembley Stadium,

BTS (pictured in 2018) played to sold out shows at London's Wembley Stadium in 2019—the first K-pop band ever to perform there. Fans worldwide have swooned over the group's smooth-cheeked good looks, boyish enthusiasm, and impeccable dance moves.

selling out shows on two consecutive nights. In 2020, during the COVID-19 pandemic, BTS hosted its first virtual concert at *Bang Bang Con: The Live*. The show drew a record-breaking online audience of 756,600 fans. In November 2022 the group became the first to garner more than 30 billion streams on Spotify.

> **"I've been part of this [BTS] fandom for nearly three years, and have engaged with it online for almost as long. Being part of this community has now become inseparable from my identity, and has been a driving force that's led to the way my life is today."[15]**
>
> **—Audrey, a devoted BTS fan**

Through all this swirl of activity, BTS's devoted fans—dubbed the ARMY, or Adorable Representative M.C. for Youth—kept up its own feverish pace on social media. ARMY is the most active fan base in K-pop, sharing comments on every possible aspect of their idols' lives and careers. In recent years, they have dealt with some shocks, as when the group announced in 2022 that it was taking a collective break so that individual members could pursue solo projects. But the ARMY's dedication to BTS shows no signs of flagging. As ARMY member Audrey says, "I've been part of this [BTS] fandom for nearly three years, and have engaged with it online for almost as long. Being part of this community has now become inseparable from my identity, and has been a driving force that's led to the way my life is today."[15]

Blackpink and the Girl Crush Concept

K-pop fans have become attached to groups that deliver a powerful message with their music. The top groups tend to have an overall motivating theme or concept that drives their creativity. For Blackpink and other K-pop girl groups, this theme is the Girl Crush concept. In general, it refers to confidence and female empowerment. Girl Crush artists see themselves as self-assured role models to their female fans. Instead of acting kittenish and cute to attract a male following, they pride themselves on a darker, edgier persona. Fashion-wise, these groups tend to favor a bad-girl image, with sexy, more adult styles that signal their independence.

A good example of Girl Crush in-your-face style is the video for Blackpink's slinky "DDU-DU DDU-DU" with its playfully bragging lyrics about financial success and independence.

From their debut in 2016, Blackpink have risen to the top by dint of hard work, multiple talents, and a message that inspires their fans to stand up for themselves. Their hard-hitting, danceable songs also tell powerful stories. The group's rappers, Lisa and Jennie, fill in the blanks for the vocalists, Rosé and Jisoo, in songs such as "How You Like That," the slow-burning "Shut Down," and "Pretty Savage." Critics have accused the group of having been carefully created to appeal to Western tastes, but their popularity among Korean fans has never wavered. All four young women in Blackpink have the talent to branch out on their own as well. Jisoo (full name: Kim Ji-soo) scored a viral hit with her lovely 2023 solo song "Flower," which drew on traditional Korean music. In October 2024, Rosé (real name: Roseanne Park) achieved her own solo milestone with the top ten single "Apt." The Melbourne, Australia, native is an example of how K-pop stars can come from anywhere.

The six-member ensemble of Everglow has rocketed to fame with their unique take on Girl Crush style. Their high-energy dance

Everglow (pictured in 2024) has rocketed to fame with their unique take on Girl Crush style. Their high-energy dance routines are ideal for live performances.

routines on numbers like "La Di Da" are ideal for live performance, as demonstrated on their Everlasting Tour of the United States and Latin America. BabyMonster, a sort of sister group to Blackpink, relies on slick vocals and aggressively sexy hip hop dancing in videos such as "Drip" and "Billionaire." Often, their intricate, precise routines are created by a team of choreographers. Like other top K-pop groups, BabyMonster creates videos that attract millions of online viewings within days—and sometimes hours—of their release.

The Rigors of K-Pop Idol Training

Such precision dance performances do not come easy. Most K-pop stars—including the members of Blackpink, Everglow, and BabyMonster—have undergone a grueling training regimen before they ever take a step onstage or in front of a camera. This method, dubbed idol training, has been used to develop the top K-pop groups since the movement's earliest days. Idol training has been examined up close in documentaries such as *Made in Korea: The K-Pop Experience* and Netflix's *Pop Star Academy: Katseye*. The latter docuseries follows twenty girls from South Korea, Japan, Australia, and the United Kingdom as they train for a year in singing, rapping, and various kinds of dancing in hopes of being chosen for the group Katseye. K-pop music companies hold auditions in Korea and in foreign countries in their search for promising talents that will appeal to audiences around the world. Their success has led corporations in other countries to conduct similar talent hunts.

A closer look at the idol training process—basically a boarding school for entertainers—has raised questions about its methods and its effects on vulnerable young performers. Some *yeonseupsaeng*, or K-pop trainees, toil for as long as five years before getting their chance to perform in public. They spend up to seventeen hours a day in the practice studio. Aside from performance skills and language instruction, they also learn about diet, exercise, fashion choices, and makeup. The managers who critique the trainees' performances pull no punches, often leaving

A Dark Side to K-Pop Stardom

According to a 2021 survey by South Korea's education ministry, primary school pupils listed singing, acting, and modeling among their top ten dream jobs. But to achieve a career in entertainment, young Koreans must survive fierce competition and grinding day-to-day pressure. In April 2023, twenty-five-year-old Moonbin, a singer, actor, and model, took his own life during a world tour with his boy band Astro. News of his death left K-pop fans in shock. It also renewed concerns about the stress placed on Korean pop stars. They face long years of training just to get started and then undergo grueling schedules and constant criticism on social media. In a society that already piles crushing demands for success on its young people, Moonbin and other young stars have succumbed to the pressure.

The flurry of young celebrity deaths in the Korean entertainment industry has led to questions about the nation's ultra-competitive culture. Some point to the unreasonable standards that pop stars must observe. "If a star behaves only a little different from what's perceived 'decent,' the public would attack them," says Korean pop culture critic Ha Jae-kun. "And it's hard for a star to ignore this kind of assault because of the high social pressure."

Quoted in Fan Wang and Yuna Ku, "Moonbin: Star's Death Renews Scrutiny on Pressures of K-Pop," BBC, April 20, 2023. www.bbc.com.

the young performers looking shell shocked or in tears. If they eventually make the final cut, the K-pop rookies can look forward to having their private lives—including dating options—subject to strict control by their music company mentors.

Blackpink's Rosé, like her fellow bandmates, underwent K-pop idol training with YG Entertainment, one of the largest agencies in South Korea. Now in her late twenties, she often reflects on the harsh system that helped her become a star. "It looked really like everyone was chasing their dreams and working so hard, but I didn't understand the lonely part," she says. "The loneliness that I would have to go through—that was a bit traumatizing. A bit shocking. But, you know, I survived it."[16]

"The loneliness that I would have to go through—that was a bit traumatizing. A bit shocking. But, you know, I survived it."[16]

—Rosé of the group Blackpink on K-pop idol training

The Future of K-Pop

Lately, several music critics have written off K-pop as a spent force in pop culture. They say that the idol factories produce cookie-cutter groups that all look and sound the same. And with top groups like BTS and Blackpink going on hiatus, they foresee a major drop-off in K-pop's popularity. Nonetheless, new groups—such as KickFlip, Verivery, NCT Wish, ILLIT, and Katseye—keep arriving on the scene each year and quickly delivering streaming favorites. Plus, as cultural critic Lee Gyu-tag observes, other countries are developing their own talent-search methods based on K-pop. "Just as hip-hop retains its identity as Black music even in the genre of Korean hip-hop," Lee says, "K-pop's identity as a Korean music genre will not disappear, even as it evolves into American K-pop or Japanese K-pop."[17]

K-Dramas and the Magic of Storytelling

Imagine an ancient hotel located in modern-day Seoul that caters only to ghosts. Its owner lives under a curse due to some long-ago crime she committed but can no longer remember. When an inquisitive young man arrives to help with the hotel's operations, he and the cursed but lovely owner find themselves falling in love. Fans of the K-drama *Hotel Del Luna* found this plotline so irresistible that it became one of the most-watched series ever on Netflix. Its popularity led to fan tours in Seoul, in which visitors could see the old hotel used as the main setting, plus some of the ghosts' clothes and props.

The writing team for the series was made up of two sisters, Hong Jung-eun and Hong Mi-ran. They have a seemingly magic touch when it comes to creating must-see TV. They followed *Hotel Del Luna* with another supernatural drama, *Alchemy of Souls*. The series, set in the imaginary land of Daeho, follows young magicians who experience twists of fate and the repercussions of forbidden magic. The Hong sisters invented so many shocking plot twists that *Alchemy of Souls*, unlike most K-dramas, was extended for a second season and a total of thirty episodes. The characters' schemes, power plays, and romantic entanglements brought a blizzard of fan comments on social media. News that the Hong sisters are planning a new series for 2025 has also been met with considerable excitement. What is their secret? As *Cosmopolitan* television critic Cianiah Kaela Apurado explains, "[The sisters] don't write separately and their two brains think as one. . . . The sisters jokingly said they fought over who would do the dishes or when they eat but never when they write scripts. This gives off very sibling energy right there!"[18]

"[The Hong sisters] don't write separately and their two brains think as one. . . . The sisters jokingly said they fought over who would do the dishes or when they eat but never when they write scripts."[18]

—Cianiah Kaela Apurado, television critic for *Cosmopolitan* magazine

The writing team of Hong Jung-eun and Hong Mi-ran created the popular supernatural drama, Alchemy of Souls*. The show's schemes, power plays, and romantic entanglements brought a blizzard of fan comments on social media.*

A Hugely Successful Cultural Export

The Hong sisters' scripts, with their wide range of stories and settings, are characteristic of K-dramas. The sisters started writing romantic comedies in the 2000s, with pun-filled dialogue and complicated, often tense situations. In 2010 they dipped into fantasy with *My Girlfriend Is a Gumiho*, about a mythical nine-tailed fox from Korean folklore. Like other K-drama creators, the Hong sisters excel at giving their audience just what it wants, along with several twists and turns viewers never anticipate.

This focus on storytelling has made K-dramas a hugely successful cultural export. Like K-pop and other Korean Wave initiatives, K-dramas have received a large boost from government support. In the 1990s the Korean government relaxed censorship standards, enabling K-dramas to explore more adult topics. It also provided subsidies and tax incentives to help production companies create new series. Over the decades, these policies resulted

Bouncing from K-Pop Idol to K-Drama Star

For the 2024 K-drama series *Doona!*, South Korean actress Bae Suzy took on the role of a troubled singer who suddenly quits the hectic world of K-pop. She moves into a sharehouse—or boarding house—to hide away and contemplate her future. There she meets a university student, played by Yang Se-jong, whose kindness and innocence sparks a romance. Playing a pop star with anxieties about fame has its challenges, but Bae could draw on personal experience. She spent seven years in the girl group Miss A, which disbanded in 2017. When asked if she had the same misgivings about the K-pop life as her character Doona, she replied, "There were moments when I was struggling, but I ignored them and still tried to be a bright and bubbly person. But Doona is different. She will let herself feel the pain and I quite admire that."

The role also calls on Bae to smoke, swear, and act terribly rude in several scenes—the opposite of her usually sweet disposition. But the actress, now approaching age thirty, likes the switch. "It was exhilarating for me," she says. "When I'm choosing a project, I think about showing a new side of me, so I was actually quite excited."

Quoted in Jan Lee, "The Life List: South Korean Actress Suzy Smokes and Swears as a Retired K-Pop Idol in *Doona!*," *Straits Times* (Toa Payoh, Singapore), November 13, 2024. www.straitstimes.com.

in an explosion of K-dramas of every description. Korean dramas have become so popular worldwide that outside sources are now anxious to bankroll them. In April 2023 Netflix pledged to devote $2.5 billion over the next four years to the production of K-dramas. Some of Netflix's most popular series ever have been K-dramas like *Squid Game*, *Alchemy of Souls*, *Extraordinary Attorney Woo*, and *Business Proposal*. And judging by the runaway 2024 hit *Queen of Tears*, the global appetite for these productions shows no sign of falling off. Among Netflix's users, more than 60 percent have sampled a K-drama. Total viewing hours for Korean shows on Netflix grew sixfold from 2019 to 2023. Hulu, Amazon Prime, and Rakuten Viki are other streaming services that have embraced K-dramas.

Critics and fans alike praise these series for their excellent production values worthy of Hollywood's best and the nuanced acting of their young stars. Crossover performers from K-pop to K-dramas also drive fans' interest, such as the singer-songwriter IU, who led the cast of *Hotel Del Luna*. Surprisingly, the language barrier has proved to be no problem for non-Korean viewers. Given the choice between subtitles and dubbed-in English dialogue, about 85 percent of Netflix consumers use subtitles when they watch K-dramas. This enables them to hear the emotional shadings of how the actors speak their lines in Korean.

Some critics attribute the success of K-dramas to more than just inventive storytelling and glossy production values. They consider the shows to be more uplifting fare compared to the cynical stories that dominate American television. Steve Choe, associate professor in the School of Cinema at San Francisco State University, believes that K-dramas' sympathetic approach can have a positive effect on viewers. He explains:

> For some, consuming K-dramas may even improve mental health through their utopian visions of community that seem more compassionate and just than our own. Their seemingly simple and often moralistic plotlines develop through unexpected and sometimes sensational twists

and turns, compelling viewers to binge-watch multiple episodes in one sitting. . . . In K-dramas such as *Stranger* and *Queen of Tears* viewers are invited to "feel the pain" of the characters and sense that they are deserving of love.[19]

Reliance on a Few Major Themes

For all their variety, K-dramas tend to rely on a few major themes that resonate with audiences—especially those in Asia that share certain cultural beliefs. One important theme is *jeong*, or human affection. This can be expressed in stories about romantic love that have lots of quirky variations. For instance, characters often meet in odd ways. In *Crash Landing on You*, a rich young businesswoman and chaebol heir accidentally paraglides into the DMZ and is rescued by a North Korean border patrol officer. But jeong also figures in plotlines about parental love, friendship, loyalty, and family ties. Sharing food and meals is usually presented as essential to social life. Many K-dramas deal with the clash between traditional values and modern urban life, with the latter often seen as a source of trouble and sorrow. This clash often results in scenes of real emotional power. Outbursts of anger or anguish are commonplace. In fact, actors in K-dramas are valued for their ability to shed tears on demand.

Another frequent theme is rags to riches, in which characters rise from the bottom of society to achieve success and happiness. In *Strongest Deliveryman*, a struggling food-delivery worker dreams of starting his own delivery app company while competing with a young woman who has her own business ambitions. *Boys Over Flowers* tells the story of a working-class girl who transfers to an elite high school and must cope with wealthy students who mostly despise her. *Business Proposal* treats the title theme as pure comedy, following an of-

> **"[K-dramas'] seemingly simple and often moralistic plotlines develop through unexpected and sometimes sensational twists and turns, compelling viewers to binge-watch multiple episodes in one sitting."[19]**
>
> —Steve Choe, associate professor in the School of Cinema at San Francisco State University

fice worker who pretends to be a wealthy society woman to go on a blind date with her company's chief executive officer.

Western viewers are likely to be struck by the influence of *han* culture on K-dramas as well. *Han* is almost untranslatable but includes dark feelings of sadness, grief, frustration, and resentment. It is often linked to Korea's historical exploitation by nearby empires in China and Japan. "*Han* not only pointed to all the sorrow and rage from the traumas inflicted on the people by historic events, but also described the unique ways in which they carried and dealt with the experiences," says Minsoo Kang, professor of history at the University of Missouri–St. Louis. "Ultimately, *han* came to signify a kind of Korean exceptionalism defined by strength and resilience in the face of inherent sadness and pain."[20] Han hovers like a dark cloud over K-dramas that deal with ghosts, family curses, and cruel fate, such as *Hotel Del Luna*.

A Runaway Sensation About Children's Games

Themes of rags to riches and cruel fate come together in the runaway K-drama hit *Squid Game*. Its debut in 2021 made it the most-watched series in the history of Netflix. It attracted 50.1 million views in its premiere week alone. Its first season has racked up more than 265 million views since its debut. Fans had to wait several years, but the second season of *Squid Game* also promised to break records. Beginning with its highly promoted release on December 26, 2024, the second season's premiere week drew 68 million views. Time will tell if the second season can garner more total views than the first one. Season 3 of *Squid Game* was scheduled for June 2025.

The premise of the series is diabolically simple. It follows several desperate people in severe financial hardship as they travel to a remote island to compete in children's games. The surviving winner among the opening 456 contestants stands to receive an enormous cash prize, equal to $31.5 million US dollars. But the losers, those who fail to complete a challenge or win a contest, meet violent deaths in various ways. Throughout the competition,

In its first season (pictured), Squid Game *was the most-watched series in Netflix history. The runaway hit series follows desperate people competing in children's games, with the winners getting rich and the losers dying gruesome deaths.*

wealthy VIPs watch the deadly games for entertainment and even wager on the contestants' life-and-death struggles.

Squid Game is not for the faint of heart. Many viewers have found its graphic violence and gore too disturbing to watch to the end. However, Hwang Dong-hyuk, the series' director and writer, says the violence and the plight of its victims are based on real-life experiences. Hwang observed a May 2009 uprising in which laid-off automobile workers occupied a SsangYong Motors factory and were shot with rubber bullets and beaten by Korean police. Hwang says one motivation in making *Squid Game* was to convey how desperate people can become. His main character, Seong Gi-hun, was based on the laid-off workers in the bloody SsangYong strikes. As Hwang says, "I wanted to show that any ordinary middle-class person in the world we live in today can fall to the bottom of the economic ladder overnight."[21]

A Triumph for the Korean Film Industry

Another political parable spiced with sudden violence became one of the biggest hits for K-cinema, or the Korean film industry.

Bong Joon-Ho's 2019 film *Parasite* follows a poor but shrewd family of grifters as they con their way into the home of a wealthy industrialist. The movie's themes of greed and class discrimination play out in unexpected ways. Like the best K-dramas, Bong's story includes shocking plot twists that force the audience to reevaluate what they have seen. *Parasite* won the top prize at the 2019 Cannes Film Festival, becoming the first Korean movie to win the award. In February 2020 the film also won the Academy Award for best picture, making it the first non-English-language film to do so. Bong took home the best director Oscar as well as shared the award for best screenplay with his cowriter, Han Jin-won. To further seal this triumph for the Korean movie industry, Bong revealed that one of his key influences was the 1960 Korean film *The Housemaid*, which long had been considered an overlooked masterpiece of world cinema.

The sudden breakthrough of *Parasite* and K-cinema in general pleased Korean film critics but also left them puzzled about the timing. For more than fifty years, South Korea had been submitting movies for Academy Award consideration with no success. Jiyoung Lee, a professor at Hankuk University of Foreign Studies, says:

"It cannot be said that cinematic perfection is the most important reason for the popularity of Korean films. There have been great [Korean] movies before. Why didn't they enjoy global popularity then and why is it possible now?"[22]

—Jiyoung Lee, professor at Hankuk University of Foreign Studies

> It cannot be said that cinematic perfection is the most important reason for the popularity of Korean films. There have been great movies before. Why didn't they enjoy global popularity then and why is it possible now? The answer requires a broader context to understand: networks that connect people around the world in real time, social media, and the expansion of platforms have made it possible for people's cultural tastes to cross national boundaries.[22]

From Genre Movies to Art-House Releases

Bong's career reflects the way K-cinema has progressed from crowd-pleasing genre movies such as comedies, thrillers, and horror flicks to more serious films. For example, in Bong's 2006 film *The Host*, an oddball family faces a hungry monster mutation that rises from the chemically contaminated Han River in Seoul. Park Chan-wook's violent thriller *Oldboy*, released in 2003, tells the story of a man who is kidnapped on the street and imprisoned for fifteen years. When finally released, he is given five days to track down his kidnapper.

Bong, Park, and other directors began to make an impression among Western film critics and art-house audiences. In Bong's tense 2009 thriller *Mother*, a woman's mentally challenged adult son is accused of murder, and she must overcome a botched investigation to clear his name. Bong's true breakthrough came with the 2014 science-fiction adventure *Snowpiercer*, about the survivors of a second ice age traveling on an endless train journey around the earth. In 2016, filmmaker Yeon Sang-ho went back to horror-film basics with *Train to Busan*, which depicts another wild train ride, this one amid a zombie apocalypse.

Cultural Tropes in K-Dramas and Movies

Anyone who watches a few Korean dramas or movies will soon notice that certain scenes or situations pop up again and again. These tropes, or plot devices, offer insights into Korean society and its core beliefs. For example, young characters treat elderly family members or other seniors with respect. This social rule goes back centuries to the teachings of Confucianism. It also accounts for other habits, such as receiving something from an older person by using both hands. Doing so is considered polite and proper.

Another trope is the after-work meeting or dinner with colleagues. These outings for drinks or meals are a cultural necessity, called *hoesik*, or eating together. They offer an opportunity for bonding and socializing, an essential part of work culture. They also include lots of drinking. In fact, K-dramas are known for frequent scenes of characters drinking too much during a crisis.

One trope that Westen moviegoers notice at once in K-dramas is the lack of physical displays of affection. Kissing or hugging in public is considered inappropriate in Korean society. Although romantic K-dramas have loosened these strictures some, characters are more likely to hold hands to demonstrate strong affection.

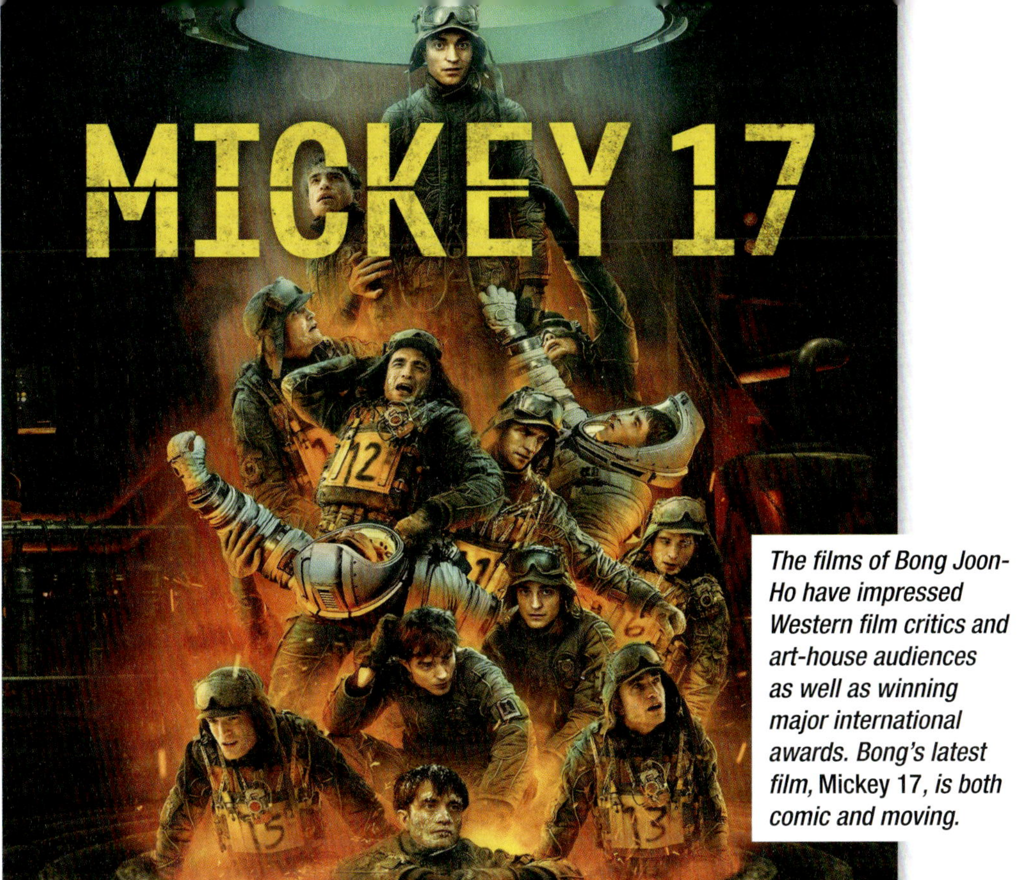

The films of Bong Joon-Ho have impressed Western film critics and art-house audiences as well as winning major international awards. Bong's latest film, Mickey 17*, is both comic and moving.*

Today Korean filmmaking faces a slump due to COVID-19-era production problems, high ticket prices, and competition from streaming and K-dramas. Gross revenues for Korean movies fell 44 percent from 2019 to 2024. However, excellent Korean films with inventive ideas continue to appear. *Concrete Utopia*, released in 2023, describes the social upheaval when an earthquake in Seoul leaves only one apartment complex standing. Its snobbish residents band together to keep outsiders from invading their safe space. *Harbin*, a historical thriller released in 2024, presents the true story of a Korean resistance fighter who assassinated Japan's prime minister in 1909. Bong's 2025 film, *Mickey 17*, is the tale of a man who signs up as an expendable assistant on dangerous space missions. Each time he dies, his body is regenerated along with most of his memories. His repeated rebirths are both comic and moving—much like the Korean films and K-dramas that have captured audiences around the world.

CHAPTER FOUR

On the Cutting Edge of World Cuisine

Americans love their Buffalo wings, especially for football watch parties and weekend get-togethers. But a new style of chicken wings has rapidly become a sensation in the United States. *Dakgangjeong*, or Korean fried chicken, has wings that are moist and crunchy, with a spicy sauce that sticks to one's fingers. Unlike most wings, the Korean wings keep their crunchiness for hours, even after they have cooled and been soaking in sauce. Their crunchy secret is that they are breaded in potato or corn starch and then fried twice at two different temperatures. The starch becomes a thin, crispy outer layer, while underneath the meat stays moist and tender. And then there are also the distinctive sauces. "It's sweet and spicy and will leave your fingers covered in an irresistible syrupy mess," says food critic Dennis Lee on the Takeout website. "I can't recommend dakgangjeong enough. This is a dish certainly worth going out of your way to get, after which you'll want to get them again and again. But remember to bring a couple of Wet-Naps for later, because you'll definitely need them."[23]

A Thriving Korean Chain with Hometown Flavor

With dishes like double-fried chicken wings, Korean chefs and food entrepreneurs are making their own contributions to Hallyu, or the Korean Wave. They share the cultural energy generated by K-pop and K-dramas. Their fresh takes on traditional dishes both inside and outside of Korea have made K-food, or Korean cuisine, popular around the world.

> "I can't recommend dakgangjeong enough. This is a dish certainly worth going out of your way to get, after which you'll want to get them again and again."[23]
>
> —Dennis Lee, Chicago-based food critic

A prime example is the thriving restaurant chain Bonchon, which is Korean for "my hometown." Launched in 2002 in Busan, South Korea, Bonchon specializes in Korean fried chicken and other dishes it refers to as Korean comfort food. Its double-frying technique was reportedly the invention of its founder, Jinduk Seo. In 2006, Jinduk opened the chain's first American restaurant in Fort Lee, New Jersey, and added a Manhattan location soon after. Today, Bonchon restaurants are found in twenty-five states, including California, Massachusetts, Texas, and Virginia. The company has a total of 455 locations around the world. Diners in Asian countries such as Philippines, Thailand, Singapore, Cambodia, and Vietnam flock to Bonchon for its signature "crunch-out-loud" fried chicken.

Prospective Bonchon franchise owners must complete a four-week training course to ensure the highest-quality food and service for each new restaurant. In addition to its signature fried

Korean fried chicken wings have become a taste sensation in the United States. They are moist and crunchy and slathered in a variety of distinctive sauces—some sweet, some spicy, and some a little bit of both.

chicken, Bonchon's menu features its version of Korean favorites such as kimchi, a spicy fermented cabbage, and bulgogi, a traditional marinated beef. Also, Bonchon has a breezy approach to marketing that fits well with Korean pop culture. Its main website says, "Bonchon Chicken is straight mukbang material. Muk-what? Muk-order-up-and-stuff-your-face deliciousness. That's what!"[24] *Mukbang* is a Korean fad for live-streamed videos that show a person eating a large amount of food at one sitting.

An Appetite for Healthy and Diverse Fare

Wolfing down a platter of fried chicken for a lark on YouTube may not be the healthiest pastime. But the rise of Korean food reflects the world's growing appetite for healthier, more diverse offerings. *Hansik*, or Korean cuisine, features lots of rice, soups, fresh vegetables, and seafood, which appeals to health-conscious diners. *Banchan*, or side dishes, tend to be high in fiber and protein and low in calories and fat. Korean recipes, of which there are thousands, come from all eight regions of the country. Each dish is made with ingredients and spices that are native to its home region, with its special geography and climate. There is an emphasis on fresh, home-grown, seasonal ingredients. Both chefs and household cooks pride themselves on balancing tastes—sour, bitter, sweet, salty, and spicy. Unlike other Asian food cultures, in which vegetables are stir-fried together, Koreans prefer to cook them separately to preserve their flavor, color, and texture. Sharing meals with family and friends is also considered essential for a healthy lifestyle. In this, Koreans draw on Confucianism and its emphasis on sharing. Confucianism is a system of moral and social philosophy that comes from ancient China.

Traditionally, Koreans view food almost the same as medicine. They think of both as having the same origin in plants and animals and thus performing quite similar functions. A proper diet is considered necessary to keep a person healthy and active. For example, kimchi, the staple side dish of fermented spicy cabbage, has been linked to longer life expectancy among South Koreans.

A K-Food Trend That Doubles as a Comfort Food

For most Koreans, *ramyeon* is an essential comfort food. These small containers of instant noodles and broth provide a quick and easy meal that never disappoints. It is important to note that ramyeon is different from Japanese noodles, or ramen. The best Korean manufacturers always use the former spelling. Ramyeon afficionados demand the genuine item, turning up their nose at brands that offer lots of salt and not much flavor. "One of my pet peeves is seeing online recipes for 'instant ramen hacks' that use these insipid varieties as a base," says Korean food writer Vivian Song. "Because for the same price, maybe a few pennies more, you can dive into a bowl of hot, spicy, soul-soothing soupy noodles in an umami-rich broth that tastes like it's been simmering for hours instead of five minutes. And the world, it seems, is catching on."

Indeed, with K-culture sweeping the world, humble but delicious ramyeon has become a trendy item. An obligatory scene in K-dramas will follow a young couple as they purchase ramyeon at a convenience store or a vending machine. A convenience store chain in Seoul, called CU Ramyun Library, actually specializes in ramyeon. Its stores have become a destination for tourists.

Vivian Song, "All About Ramyeon, the Korean Comfort Food That's More than Just a Trend," The Takeout, January 1, 2022. www.thetakeout.com.

The healthful quality of hansik is aligned with so-called temple food, what monks and nuns eat every day at Buddhist temples in South Korea. Temple food includes no meat or artificial flavorings. Pungent herbs such as onions, garlic, leeks, and chives are also prohibited. Temple occupants perform every step of preparing meals, from cultivating the gardens and fields to cooking the rice and vegetables. Temple food, however, need not be bland or boring. Balwoo Gongyang, a temple-influenced fine-dining restaurant in Seoul, has earned top marks from upscale rating services like Michelin. It attracts diners from around the world.

The Spread of K-Food and High-End Korean Restaurants

Energized by the Korean Wave, high-end restaurants serving K-food are becoming a global phenomenon. Many of them are also winning awards for their innovative menus. Korean chefs like Junghyun Park, known as JP, have been training and developing their skills in the kitchen since the early 2000s. Now their hard work and new ideas are paying off with breakthrough restaurants. Park and his wife, Ellia, own four restaurants in New York, including Atomix, whose cuisine has earned it a place on the World's 50 Best Restaurants list. Park insists that he does not have to worry about adapting his high-end K-food dishes to American palates. He simply focuses on what tastes good. "I like cooking in New York because people there are very open to new cultures," says Park. "They like accepting new things. So it's not like I have to change their tastes."[25]

Atomix offers a ten-course sampler of traditional Korean dishes with an artful twist. A bowl of seaweed soup is flavored with pork broth and cuts of sea urchin from Hokkaido, Japan. A simple potato pancake becomes a delicious, crispy side dish topped with ricotta cheese. Yellowtail sashimi, or thinly sliced raw fish, is raised to something sublime with the addition of spicy fermented carrots. The Parks hope their K-food innovations inspire other

A simple Korean-style potato pancake (pictured) becomes a delectable side dish in the hands of chef Junghyun Park, whose artful twists on traditional Korean cooking have won prestigious awards and the adoration of food lovers in the United States.

up-and-coming chefs. “Our first goal was to open our small restaurants well,” says Ellia. “Now our goal is legacy, the legacy of our culture in this country and of the next generation.”[26]

Koreans visiting K-food restaurants in New York, Paris, or London often point out how comfort food dishes from home, valued for their low cost and ease of preparation, are served as high-priced items in the big city. At Jua, a Korean restaurant in New York’s trendy Flatiron District, a humble *gimbap*, or seaweed roll, is piled high with caviar to make it a luxury item. Most Koreans prefer the simpler version and memories of eating such food as children on their grandmother’s couch. “A bowl of *naengmyeon* (cold buckwheat noodles) is more delicious under a rattling fan,” notes food and travel writer Lee Jian, “and late-night bibimbap [a rice bowl dish] should be whipped up with whatever *banchan* (side dishes) are left in the fridge.”[27]

The Funky Charm of Korean Street Food

The funky, communal side of K-food finds its best expression in Korean street food. Some of the most innovative dishes are prepared in street food markets in Korean cities and towns. People gather at these street markets to stroll around and sample offerings from food trucks and booths. At the same time, they share news and gossip, listen to music, catch up with old friends, and meet new ones as well. Street markets also provide the perfect setting for Korea’s food-sharing culture. Couples and families are eager to share bites of whatever delicious dish they have discovered.

One of the top destinations for street food in South Korea is the Gwangjang Market in Seoul. Dating back to 1905, Gwangjang has been operating in much the same way for decades. Although originally known for its clothing and handicrafts, it has become an essential stop for visitors who want to investigate the amazing variety of street food in Korea. The market is lined with stalls displaying mounds of food, while hungry-looking customers check out the choices. While upscaled in foreign restaurants, the gimbap, a rice roll with meat and pickled vegetables rolled up in seaweed, is a common inexpensive find. Cut into bite-sized pieces, it is ideal for sharing. There are also mung bean pancakes, dumplings, and *kalguksu*, which is a light, refreshing noodle soup.

Korean street food vendors in America pride themselves on combining traditional Korean fare with tastes from other cultures. The result is food fusions like kimchi tacos and burritos filled with bibimbap, or rice, beef, sauteed vegetables, and spicy chili paste. Korean American chef Roy Choi is a legend among Korean street food fans. Choi led the food truck movement in 2008 with dishes that blend Korean and Mexican flavors. Kogi BBQ, Choi's most famous creation, consists of taco shells filled with chunks of spicy Korean short ribs. His gourmet Korean Mexican taco trucks changed the landscape for street food in Los Angeles. "Although maybe a larger society wasn't eating at food trucks the same way they do now, it is a cultural thing," says Choi. "It comes from neighborhoods, it comes from immigrants and it comes from people that I grew up around. It is a very important resource and a way to become an American."[28]

"Although maybe a larger society wasn't eating at food trucks the same way they do now, it is a cultural thing. It comes from neighborhoods, it comes from immigrants and it comes from people that I grew up around."[28]

—Roy Choi, Korean American chef and food truck entrepreneur

Hungry patrons wait to place their orders at chef Roy Choi's Kogi Taqueria food truck in Los Angeles in 2022. Choi's most famous creation consists of taco shells filled with chunks of spicy Korean short ribs.

Chef's "Seoul Food" Dishes Combine Tastes from Two Cultures

Korean-fusion cooking comes naturally to LaMara Davidson. The daughter of an African American soldier and his Korean wife, Davidson grew up with foods from two distinct cultures. Her grandmother and aunts loved to cook collard greens and other southern dishes, a skill they passed along to Davidson's mom. Eventually, Davidson also learned the fine points of Korean cooking. She especially values her mother's hands-on approach in the kitchen. "We made kimchi together a couple of years ago and every time she needed to add chili and salt sugar, I poured it in her hands over the bowl," says Davidson. "We put our hearts into the food we share with others, but I didn't fully understand how our hands were the most important tools."

Davidson has combined her two main influences to forge a sparkling career as a chef. A few years of culinary training in New York and Paris gave her confidence to set out on her own. She calls her fresh takes on southern and Korean comfort foods "Seoul food." Her trademark Cornbread & Kimchi cooking style has drawn rave reviews from food critics and home cooks alike. As she confides today, "I consider myself an artist when it comes to food especially."

Quoted in Tiffani Rozier, "Chef LaMara Davidson on Fusing Her African American and Korean Heritage to Create 'Seoulfood,'" *Essence*, January 7, 2022. www.essence.com.

Finding Success with BBQ in a Cup

Another food truck sensation has turned into the latest K-food success story in America. Cupbop, a K-food franchise, began in Provo, Utah, as a food truck menu item. A Korean immigrant named Jung Song was serving Korean barbecued beef and rice in a cup for the convenience of office workers. Dok Kwon, who was also a Korean immigrant, happened to work as a government accountant in the office building across from Jung's food truck. Dok loved Jung's food, and when Dok was transferred to New York City, he urged Jung to move there as well. Instead, Jung started Cupbop and within a few years had opened ten Cupbop restaurants. Dok had stayed in touch and became obsessed with the idea that he could make Cupbop into something truly special. "I thought, 'how cool would this be if I'm the very first person to help create a national Korean brand in the United States,'" recalls Dok. "That's something nobody's done, nobody."[29]

> "Korean cuisine's allure extends far beyond taste. It's a complete sensory experience, that tantalizes the eyes, the taste buds, and the soul. . . . This culinary diversity, combined with the nation's growing global influence, has made K-food a sensation worldwide."[30]
>
> —Simon N. Meade-Palmer, technology and creativity writer

In May 2022 Dok and Jung took their case for the franchise's bright future to the financial TV show *Shark Tank*. There they convinced billionaire Mark Cuban to invest a million dollars in Cupbop in exchange for 5 percent ownership. The result has been a triumph for both the business and K-food in general. Their street-food-style barbecue and other Korean favorites have won over customers across the United States and in Indonesia. By December 2024 Cupbop had expanded to 260 locations, with more on the way.

Creative K-food businesses and restaurants continue to spread the word about Korean cuisine. Social media sites like YouTube and Instagram introduce Korean recipes and cooking styles to millions of foodies each year. "Korean cuisine's allure extends far beyond taste," says Simon N. Meade-Palmer, who writes on technology and creativity. "It's a complete sensory experience, that tantalizes the eyes, the taste buds, and the soul. The sweet, spicy, savoury, and umami [meaty] notes, harmonize beautifully in dishes such as bulgogi, kimchi, bibimbap, and Korean barbecue. This culinary diversity, combined with the nation's growing global influence, has made K-food a sensation worldwide."[30]

CHAPTER FIVE

The Rise of K-Fashion and a Skin Care Empire

During the first week of January 2025, South Korea's superstar designers unveiled their new designs in the fashion and culture festival Runway to Seoul. The show featured a mixture of K-fashion, K-pop, and technology, demonstrating the energy and far-reaching potential of the Korean fashion industry. More than twenty-five hundred attendees, including global influencers like Australia's Eunice Wani, took part in the swirling festivities. Among the seven top design houses on hand were Mina Chung, Duckdive, Tripleroot, and Re Rhee. Helping keep the street vibe alive were H1-Key, a K-pop girl group, and the dance crew We Dem Boyz. Even the venue for the event had its own ultramodern style. The Dongdaemun Design Plaza, created by world-renowned architect Zaha Hadid, is Seoul's futuristic masterpiece. The enormous building looks like a curving, glittering spaceship that has landed in the heart of a bustling shopping district.

The second annual Runway to Seoul event made a strong case for the Korean Wave's continuing influence on fashion and culture. High-tech photo booths and artificial reality installations added to the modernist feel. Organizers hinted that Seoul could soon rival Paris and New York as a hub for high fashion. "Runway to Seoul is a unique cultural festival born from the fusion of K-fashion, K-pop, and technology," says Hyunwoo Kim, chief executive officer of the Seoul Business Agency. "It goes beyond being a fashion show, revealing the potential and creativity of K-fashion to the world, contributing to its strengthened presence in the global market."[31]

Promoting Fashion Designs with K-Pop Stars

A new music video or photoshoot by a K-pop star offers a designer the perfect opportunity to reach a young audience. K-fashion labels use the worldwide popularity of Korean pop culture to promote their fashion designs to sharp-eyed fans. When Blackpink's Jennie (full name: Jennie Kim) wears brand-new geometric-shaped eyeglasses, for example, her fans are sure to want their own pair. Jennie's collaboration with Gentle Monster (GM), a hip South Korean eyewear brand, has set a new standard for global fashion partnerships. GM gives its creations for Jennie playful pastel colors to attract younger customers. It also makes accessories for each pair of glasses, such as detachable charms with bows and hearts.

Fashion labels such as the hip South Korean eyewear brand Gentle Monster have paired with K-pop stars like Blackpink's Jennie (pictured). Partnerships like this have set a new standard for global fashion.

Sampling the Fashion Districts of Seoul

Visitors who enjoy shopping for fashionable clothes have lots of options in Seoul. Several distinct neighborhoods have their own vibe and sense of style. Myeondong is a busy shopping district that offers everything from the highest-end labels to the funkiest, quirkiest boutiques. While dodging the crowds in Myeondong, shoppers can also find street vendors hawking a variety of K-beauty products. For luxury shopping, Gangnam is Seoul's centerpiece. Ritzy department stores and designer boutiques carry the latest Korean styles and global brands. For travelers on a budget, Gangnam is a fun place simply to people watch and keep an eye out for K-pop stars.

With its focus on streetwise style and pockets of high fashion, the Apgujeong neighborhood offers a visual feast for visitors. A stroll down the street is like walking into a fashion magazine, with high-style diners filling the outdoor cafés. Hidden away on the side streets are shops filled with the trendiest K-fashions. Finally, the Hongdae district offers an eclectic mix of indie shops, pop-up boutiques, flea markets, and hangouts for artsy young people. It might be the best option for finding some local designer's unique creation for a surprisingly low price.

To deliver an uncommon shopping experience, GM has set up temporary pop-up stores for die-hard fans. Jentle Home, a pop-up store inspired by Jennie's childhood, allowed customers to try on eyewear as they immersed themselves in the singer's life story. The 2024 Jentle Salon pop-up store added hair accessories to Jennie's latest eyewear collection. Fans who share their shopping experience on Instagram and other social media help spread the excitement. "K-pop idols are not just performers but fashion icons who have bridged music and fashion in the creative industry," says New York attorney Seoryung Park, an expert in fashion law. "Social media has amplified their influence, allowing direct interaction with fans and fostering loyal communities that promote their fashion."[32] Park says Jennie's partnership with GM showcases Korea's growing influence on global fashion. Jennie has also become a regular at Paris Fashion Week and has led ad campaigns for global brands such as Chanel and Calvin Klein.

Designers and K-pop stars also share the spotlight during Seoul Fashion Week (SFW), another annual Korean fashion event. In the February 2024 SFW, K-pop stars not only had front-row seats for runway presentations, they also met with some of the fashion industry's standout designers. The group NewJeans served as official ambassadors for the five-day event. Since launching their group in July 2022, NewJeans's five members have already signed deals with fashion heavyweights such as Gucci, Armani, Louis Vuitton, and Levi's. The band has also done photo shoots with *American Vogue*. Their inviting mid-tempo musical style seems to mesh with fashion styles that are simple and streetwise, such as cropped T-shirts, oversize sweatshirts, and baggy cargo pants.

"K-pop and fashion in K-pop are really blowing up around the world. Fashion is important to artistry, for artists to stand out onstage. The popularity of K-pop and events like [Seoul Fashion Week] really help introduce a lot of Korean designers to the world."[33]

—Brian, member of the K-pop duo Fly to the Sky

SFW has become a must-see exhibition for designers, buyers, and fashion editors not only in Asia but around the world. The K-pop connections ensure that the event will explode each year on social media. "K-pop and fashion in K-pop are really blowing up around the world. Fashion is important to artistry, for artists to stand out onstage," says Brian of the K-pop duo Fly to the Sky. He adds, "The popularity of K-pop and events like [SFW] really help introduce a lot of Korean designers to the world."[33]

A Homecoming for Art and Cutting Edge Fashion

South Korea's most innovative designers tend to blur the boundary between art and business. Longtime friends Jessica Jung and Dami Kwon created their design house We11done with an artistic vision in mind. They consider their fashion creations to be like fabric sculptures, with an emphasis on graceful silhouettes and gender-neutral styles. Several years ago, the pair moved to Paris to pursue their vision. But the cultural energy of K-pop and K-fashion drew them back to Seoul in 2023. Since moving back, Jung has embraced her Korean roots in her designs. For We11done's 2024 collection, she found inspiration in the work of Korean sculptor Do Ho Suh, as well as memories of her suburban childhood in South Korea.

Jung and Kwon staged their comeback fashion show, Remnants of Home, at an art fair called Frieze Seoul near the upscale COEX Mall in Gangnam. The site is linked to K-pop videos and Korean Wave extravagance. "COEX symbolizes K-pop, and because We11done pursues and is inspired by art, it made sense to show during Frieze Seoul," says Jung, who serves as the brand's creative director. "Although K-pop isn't a direct inspiration for us, the Korean culture and trends represented by it are. . . . It feels good to be home."[34]

The show was a hit from the first model's stroll down the elegant white chute in a sleeveless vinyl dress. Cheers erupted with the appearance of each new design. In keeping with the theme of childhood memories, some dresses looked like a wrapped child's blanket, while others resembled the crinkly white silhouettes of paper dolls. Jung admits that her ideas can come from anywhere. "[The inspiration] can be a music video, a film or a TV show," she says.

The designs of Jessica Jung and Dami Kwon are on display at the We11done Menswear show during Paris Fashion Week in January 2020. The pair created their design house, We11done, with an artistic vision in mind.

"I always begin with a simple form and then explore the thoughts it triggers; we're continuing to choose art as the starting point of our collections."[35]

"[The inspiration] can be a music video, a film or a TV show. I always begin with a simple form and then explore the thoughts it triggers; we're continuing to choose art as the starting point of our collections."[35]

—Jessica Jung, Korean fashion designer for We11done

Jung and Kwon's homecoming in Seoul occurred just as the Korean Wave was expanding their country's influence globally. The two friends admit to being amazed at Korea's sudden cultural rise. "As a Korean, when we were kids, we actually never imagined our culture getting this kind of attention from the world," says Jung. "We always admired Western culture, Hollywood films. But nowadays, Korean pop culture is really the core of worldwide pop culture. We say that this is really ironic because Korea is traditional, too."[36]

K-Beauty and the Desire for Glass Skin

Just as K-pop and K-dramas have energized Korean fashion, they have also helped make Korean beauty products popular worldwide. So called K-beauty, or Korean skin care, has become the standard against which products from other nations are measured. K-pop stars, and not just the females, strive to maintain so-called glass skin. Their skin is so healthy and well hydrated that it looks clear, smooth, and radiant like glass. Pores are almost invisible. This luminous appearance is often achieved even without makeup. Close-ups of K-idols in videos and dramas generally do not need to be digitally tweaked to eliminate rough or red patches of skin. Young faces seem to glow with a translucence that fans desperately want for themselves. To achieve the glass skin look, many young people turn to skin care products manufactured in Korea, such as those made by Dr.Jart+ and Innisfree. Customers can find them at American beauty outlets like Sephora. They can also shop for products that suit their specific skin type and needs.

All sorts of K-beauty trends and innovations have revolutionized the global market for skin care. Sheet masks, slugging, and multistep skin care have been praised and debated endlessly on social media. Fashion magazines and websites dive into the details of these products and treatments to explain how to use them and why they are effective.

For example, a sheet mask is a thin, fabric-like covering that is soaked in serums containing vitamins and minerals. When applied to the face for a few minutes, the mask refreshes the skin with moisture and nutrients. Slugging is the application of a layer of petroleum jelly to the skin and leaving it overnight. When removed, the treatment leaves a slimy residue, like the trail of a slug. The ten-step skin care routine is designed so that each step nourishes the skin in a particular way. The ritual, which is time consuming, includes double cleansing to remove dirt and makeup; applying essence, or a watery, textured product for extra hydration; and using serums, sheet masks, and moisturizers to give the face a supple appearance. Many young Koreans—and their counterparts around the world—have become amateur experts on these methods in their quest for flawless skin.

All sorts of Korean beauty trends and innovations have revolutionized the global market for skin care. Sheet masks (shown)—thin, fabric-like coverings that are soaked in serums containing vitamins and minerals—are one.

Finding Global Success with Marketing and Social Media

K-beauty companies excel at promoting their skin care products in innovative ways, including through endorsements by K-pop celebrities. But the companies also make outstanding products that they are constantly trying to improve. Distinctive ingredients from Korea such as snail mucin, birch sap, ginseng, fermented rice water, and honey give K-beauty products like toners and essences an authentic back-to-nature feel. Not only are the products known for their high quality, they also have lower prices than competitors in the West. And their affordable excellence is producing a cascade of revenue. Experts at GlobalData, a British analytics firm, predict that the beauty market in South Korea will be worth more than $21 billion by 2026. South Korea has also become the top exporter of beauty products to the United States.

The promise of glass skin is a marketer's dream, and K-beauty firms specialize in the use of social media and influencers to spread the word about their products. A community of users worldwide share their experiences with K-beauty on Instagram, YouTube, TikTok, and other platforms. On Instagram alone, the hashtag #Kbeauty leads to thousands of stories about skin care rituals, preferred products, and before-and-after successes. These user testimonials represent marketing gold.

TikTok also makes major contributions to K-beauty's success. Marketing expert Daniel Jeon says K-beauty brands are using a two-platform online strategy that is revolutionary. "They create buzz on TikTok, where Gen Z spends countless hours discovering new products, and then seamlessly direct this interest to Amazon for easy purchasing," says Jeon. "Unlike traditional advertising, these genuine testimonials from trusted influencers carry unprecedented weight with younger consumers."[37]

"[K-beauty companies] create buzz on TikTok, where Gen Z spends countless hours discovering new products, and then seamlessly direct this interest to Amazon for easy purchasing. . . . Unlike traditional advertising, these genuine testimonials from trusted influencers carry unprecedented weight with younger consumers."[37]

—Daniel Jeon, marketing expert

A Surprising Survey of Korean Skin Care Products

Rosa Jisoo Pyo thought she knew pretty much everything about Korean skin care long before it became an obsession in her adopted country, the United States. Her mom wore facial sheet masks, swore by ginseng and snail cream cleansers, and slugged and moisturized faithfully. Pyo thought of her supposed expertise in skin care as her lifeline to her native Korean culture. "Not only am I using Korean skin care," she told herself, "but I'm using good Korean skin care, like the créme de la créme of sunscreen, Beauty of Joseon."

However, a trip to Seoul proved to Pyo how wrong she had been. She visited Olive Young, the top beauty chain in Korea, and was surprised that nothing on the shelves looked familiar. A store clerk at Olive Young had never heard of Pyo's favorite Beauty of Joseon sunscreen. Instead, she suggested several sunscreens considered to be the absolute best. Pyo soon discovered brand-new options for skin prep, skin masking, and moisturizers. Snail mucin, which was the hottest skin care item in the United States, had been replaced in Korea by more effective treatments years before. Pyo left Olive Young with a bag full of cutting edge beauty products and a new respect for Korean technology in skin care.

Rosa Jisoo Pyo, "My Trip to Korea Taught Me the Truth About Skin Care," The Cut, April 10, 2023. www.thecut.com.

Marketing K-beauty products is also boosted by their distinctive packaging. Korean skin care products catch the buyer's eye with packaging that can be sleek and elegant or playful and whimsical. Peach & Lily's Marine Jewel Capsule for face serum looks like a translucent jewelry case with a golden fish on top. Tony Moly sells its Minion Aromatherapy Eucalyptus Calming Stick in a bright yellow tube with a face and eyeglasses, like the Minions from the *Despicable Me* movies. Such packaging conveys the vibrant ideas that make the Korean Wave so much fun for consumers.

A Commitment to Style and Culture

K-fashion's streetwise designs and the everyday elegance of K-beauty products have helped Korean companies become world leaders in style and culture. Designers and product developers have plugged in to the energy of K-pop to express their vision for the future. It will be fascinating to see what surprises Hallyu has in store for the world in years to come.

SOURCE NOTES

Introduction: A Newly Energized Pop Culture

1. Quoted in Karin, "Dressing Up in the Glow of K-Dramas: Fashion Inspiration and Beauty Trends," Medium, March 25, 2024. https://kibinkakushite.medium.com.
2. Quoted in Afeeya Akhand, "Distinguishing Between Soft Power and Propaganda in South Korean Foreign Policy," The Strategist, March 21, 2023. www.aspistrategist.org.
3. Jack Neighbour, "Korea, What's Next?," *National Geographic*, January 16, 2024. www.nationalgeographic.com.

Chapter One: Riding the Korean Wave

4. Quoted in MFA Boston, "Museum of Fine Arts, Boston, Hosts U.S. Debut of Hallyu! The Korean Wave," February 29, 2024. www.mfa.org.
5. Quoted in Tim Adams, "K-Everything: The Rise and Rise of Korean Culture," *The Guardian* (Manchester, UK), September 4, 2022. www.theguardian.com.
6. Euny Hong, "How South Korea Became the Capital of Pop Culture," *Allure*, April 13, 2020. www.allure.com.
7. Quoted in *Taipei Times* (Taipei, Taiwan), "'Gangnam Style' Breaks 1 Billion YouTube Views," December 23, 2012. www.taipeitimes.com.
8. Quoted in Qasim Nauman, "'Gangnam Style' Impact Endures a Decade After It Broke the Internet," *Barron's*, July 11, 2022. www.barrons.com.
9. Adams, "K-Everything."
10. Quoted in Min Jeong Lee and Sangmi Cha, "South Korea's 'Hurry Hurry' Culture Helps Bring Down a President," Bloomberg, December 17, 2024. www.bloomberg.com.

Chapter Two: The Explosion of K-Pop

11. Quoted in Shannon Power, "Taylor Swift's Viral K-Pop Photo Leaves People 'Crying,'" *Newsweek*, March 4, 2024. www.newsweek.com.
12. Quoted in Power, "Taylor Swift's Viral K-Pop Photo Leaves People 'Crying.'"
13. Los Angeles Film School, "A Brief History of K-Pop," 2021. www.lafilm.

14. Tiffany Yep, "BTS Songs That Address Social Issues," Pop Tokki, September 25, 2023. www.poptokki.com.
15. Audrey, "BTS, ARMY, and Online Engagement as a Force for Social Good," Medium, March 8, 2022. https://anticurseantihero.medium.com.
16. Quoted in Lulu Garcia-Navarro, "The Interview: K-Pop Trained Rosé to Be 'a Perfect Girl.' Now She's Trying to Be Herself," *New York Times*, November 23, 2024. www.nytimes.com.
17. Quoted in Se Eun Gong, "Why K-Pop's Future Is in Crisis, According to Its Chief Guardian," NPR, April 8, 2023. www.npr.org.

Chapter Three: K-Dramas and the Magic of Storytelling

18. Cianiah Kaela Apurado, "Love 'Alchemy of Souls'? Here Are 5 Must-Watch K-Dramas Written by the Same Writer," *Cosmopolitan*, August 14, 2022. www.cosmo.ph.
19. Steve Choe, "Sympathy for the K-Drama," *Georgetown Journal of International Affairs*, June 11, 2024. https://gjia.georgetown.edu.
20. Minsoo Kang, "The Problem with 'Han,'" *Aeon*, March 18, 2022. https://aeon.co.
21. Quoted in Claire Lee, "The Real-Life Violence That Inspired South Korea's 'Squid Game,'" *Barron's*, December 23, 2024. www.barrons.com.
22. Quoted in Kim Jae-Ha, "A Brief History of K-Cinema," V&A, September 24, 2022. www.vam.ac.uk.

Chapter Four: On the Cutting Edge of World Cuisine

23. Dennis Lee, "Why Korean Chicken Wings Are Some of the Best on Earth," The Takeout, July 6, 2022. www.thetakeout.com.
24. Bonchon, "Our Story: Welcome to Bonchon," 2025. www.bonchon.com.
25. Quoted in Anthony Kuhn, "Korean Food Is Winning Over Palates Worldwide, Including the World of Haute Cuisine," *Morning Edition*, NPR, January 25, 2024. www.npr.org.
26. Quoted in Elyse Inamine, "Atomix Made Them Stars. Where Do They Go from Here? JP and Ellia Park Are Starting to Think Beyond Restaurants," Grub Street, May 23, 2023. www.grubstreet.com.
27. Lee Jian, "'You Can't Get This in Korea': K-Food Finds a New, Upscale Identity in New York City," *Korea JoongAng Daily*, May 30, 2024. https://koreajoongangdaily.joins.com.
28. Quoted in Sarah Mosqueda, "Chef Roy Choi Talks Struggles, Successes and Living in O.C.," *Los Angeles Times*, July 17, 2024. www.latimes.com.

29. Quoted in Lee Benson, "How Two Korean Immigrants Turned Cupbop into a National Sensation," *Deseret News* (Salt Lake City, UT), February 26, 2023. www.deseret.com.
30. Simon N. Meade-Palmer, "K-Cuisine: Bridging Tradition and Technology in Culinary Delights," *Technopreneurship360* (blog), August 5, 2024. https://technopreneurship360.com.

Chapter Five: The Rise of K-Fashion and a Skin Care Empire

31. Quoted in PR Newswire, "Showcasing the Vibrant Lifestyle of Seoul: 2024 Runway to Seoul," January 8, 2025. www.prnewswire.com.
32. Seoryung Park, "K-Pop Idols as Fashion Idols: How Artist Collaborations Influence Design Trends," *Fashion & Law Journal*, June 13, 2024. https://fashionlawjournal.com.
33. Quoted in Lee Hyo-won, "Seoul Fashion Week Faces Growing Pains," *Women's Wear Daily*, February 12, 2024. https://wwd.com.
34. Quoted in Gennady Oreshkin, "Jessica and Dami Kwon of We11done on Their Return to Seoul," *Prestige*, October 11, 2023. www.prestigeonline.com.
35. Quoted in Oreshkin, "Jessica and Dami Kwon of We11done on Their Return to Seoul."
36. Quoted in Gloria Tso, "How Seoul-Based Avant-Garde Brand We11done Carves Its Niche: Style Chats to Co-founder Jessica Jung About Identity, Blurring Boundaries Between Fashion and Art, and More—Interview," *South China Morning Post* (Hong Kong), December 15, 2023. www.scmp.com.
37. Daniel Jeon, "Korean Cosmetics Marketing Strategy: Dominate TikTok like K-Beauty's Leaders," Spray: Marketing Insight, February 10, 2025. https://boost.spray.io.

FOR FURTHER RESEARCH

Books

Simon Clair, *K Culture: K-Pop, Cuisine, On Screen, and More—Celebrating the Korean Wave*. London: Quadrille, 2023.

Hallyu, *The K-Pop Phenomenon: Origins, Evolution, and Future—Trace the History of First to Fifth-Generation Idols; Explore the Forces Behind the Global Sensation*. Hallyu, 2024.

Karen Han, *Bong Joon Ho: Dissident Cinema*. New York: Abrams, 2022.

Mukbang Mike Horan, *Korean Street Food Made Easy (Exploring the Wonders of Korean Cuisine)*. Self-published, 2025.

Grace Jung, *K-Drama School: A Pop Culture Inquiry into Why We Love Korean Television*. Philadelphia, PA: Running Press, 2024.

Stuart A. Kallen, *K-Pop: The Music Sensation Sweeping the Globe*. San Diego, CA: Referencepoint, 2025.

Lilin Yang et al., *The Korean Skincare Bible: The Ultimate Guide to K-Beauty Secrets*. London: Cassell, 2019.

Internet Sources

Lyla Abbas, "Why Korean Skincare Has Taken the World by Storm," Tribune Wired, March 17, 2024. www.tribunewired.com.

Sanya Anand and David Sehyeon Baek, "Understanding Hallyu: The Impact of Korean Pop Culture," Marketing Journal, March 13, 2024. www.marketingjournal.org.

Jack Neighbour, "Korea, What's Next?," *National Geographic*, January 16, 2024. www.nationalgeographic.com.

Laura Toyryla, "K-Drama—the Ultimate Guide to Best Korean Dramas, Genres, and Must-Watch Shows in 2025," *90 Day Korean* (blog), February 20, 2025. www.90daykorean.com.

Jin Yu Young, "If It Isn't Perfect, Is It Still K-Pop?," *New York Times*, January 30, 2024. www.nytimes.com.

Websites

allkpop

www.allkpop.com

Launched in 2007 by Korean Americans Johnny Noh and Paul Han, allkpop is the largest English language website for K-pop news and facts in the world. It provides a continuous stream of up-to-the-minute information on K-pop groups, music releases, and live shows.

Asia Society

https://asiasociety.org

Asia Society is a nonprofit and nonpartisan organization that seeks to promote mutual understanding and strengthen partnerships among peoples, leaders, and institutions of Asia and the United States. Founded in 1956 in New York, Asia Society has sponsored many projects that involve South Korea, including the Korean Wave Initiative.

Foxylab New York

https://foxylabny.com

Foxylab New York describes itself as a creative laboratory that merges art and fashion. Its online magazine serves as a go-to source for inspiration and discovery of creative talents. Its website features interviews with fashion leaders and articles on fashion trends. K-fashion trends are one of the main topics on Foxylab New York.

Korean Cultural Center

https://washingtondc.korean-culture.org

The Korean Cultural Center in Washington, DC, seeks to introduce South Korean culture to Americans and expand cultural exchange between the two nations. It presents a variety of events during the year. All About That Hallyu Com-On is the center's annual celebration of Korean pop culture, with guest performances, activities, and fan community meetups.

90 Day Korean

www.90daykorean.com

90 Day Korean is a blog and social media channel dedicated to providing information about Korean language and culture. Its team of native Koreans and foreigners who live in Korea strive to make Korean language learning fun, easy, and practical. They also try to foster cultural understanding and ideas of global citizenship.

INDEX

PICTURE CREDITS

Cover: K-Angle/Shutterstock

5: TCD/Prod.DB /Alamy Stock Photo
9: PHOTOPQR/LE PARISIEN/Newscom
12: Seokyong Lee/BlackStar Photos/Newscom
16: Doug Peters/Alamy Stock Photo
19: UPI/Alamy Stock
22: Associated Press
24: Yonhap News/YNA/Newscom
29: TVN/Album/Newscom
34: Album/Alamy Stock Photo
37: WARNER BROS./Album/Newscom
39: DronG/Shutterstock
42: Let Geo Create/Shutterstock
44: fivetonine/Shutterstock
48: yllyso/Shutterstock
51: Sipa USA via AP
53: Kateryna Onyshchuk/Alamy Stock Photo